AF269443

RUSSIA

R.L. Van

Big Buddy Books
An Imprint of Abdo Publishing
abdobooks.com

abdobooks.com

Published by Abdo Publishing, a division of ABDO, PO Box 398166, Minneapolis, Minnesota 55439.
Copyright © 2023 by Abdo Consulting Group, Inc. International copyrights reserved in all countries. No part of this book may be reproduced in any form without written permission from the publisher. Big Buddy Books™ is a trademark and logo of Abdo Publishing.

Printed in the United States of America, North Mankato, Minnesota
102022
012023

Design: Emily O'Malley, Mighty Media, Inc.
Production: Mighty Media, Inc.
Editor: Jessica Rusick
Cover Photograph: V_E/Shutterstock Images
Interior Photographs: andriano.cz/Shutterstock Images, p. 6 (top); Anton Watman/Shutterstock Images, p. 6 (middle); AP Images, p. 21; BearFotos/Shutterstock Images, p. 19; cliplab/Shutterstock Images, p. 26 (right); Drop of Light/Shutterstock Images, p. 29 (bottom); Ella Shin/Shutterstock Images, p. 26 (left); Everett Collection/Shutterstock Images, p. 28 (top); Filip Bjorkman/Shutterstock Images, p. 7 (map); Free Wind 2014/Shutterstock Images, p. 9; Katvic/Shutterstock Images, p. 25; lukulo/iStockphoto, pp. 5 (compass), 7 (compass); MaciejGillert/Shutterstock Images, p. 23; Maksim Safaniuk/Shutterstock Images, p. 17; mark reinstein/Shutterstock Images, p. 11; Maxim Petrichuk/Shutterstock Images, p. 27 (bottom); NASA/Wikimedia Commons, p. 28 (bottom); Nataliya Borysenko/Shutterstock Images, p. 30 (flag); pudiq/Shutterstock Images, p. 13; Pyty/Shutterstock Images, p. 5 (map); Serg Zastavkin/Shutterstock Images, p. 6 (bottom); Sergey Petrov/Shutterstock Images, p. 27 (top right); Thirteen/Shutterstock Images, p. 30 (currency); V_E/Shutterstock Images, p. 27 (top left); VarnakovR/Shutterstock Images, p. 15; Vitaliy Ankov/AP Images, p. 29 (top)
Design Elements: Mighty Media, Inc.
Country population and area figures taken from the CIA World Factbook

Library of Congress Control Number: 2022940507

Publisher's Cataloging-in-Publication Data
Names: Van, R.L., author.
Title: Russia / by R.L. Van
Description: Minneapolis, Minnesota : Abdo Publishing, 2023 | Series: Countries | Includes online resources and index.
Identifiers: ISBN 9781532199721 (lib. bdg.) | ISBN 9781098274924 (ebook)
Subjects: LCSH: Russia--Juvenile literature. | Europe--Juvenile literature. | Russia--History--Juvenile literature. | Geography--Juvenile literature.
Classification: DDC 947--dc23

CONTENTS

PASSPORT TO RUSSIA

Russia is a country in both Europe and Asia. It is the largest country in the world by area. More than 142 million people live there.

DID YOU KNOW?

The Russian language uses different letters than English. In Russian, the word *Russia* is spelled Россия.

WHERE IS RUSSIA?
Arctic Ocean
N
W E
S
RUSSIA
Kazakhstan
Mongolia
China
Pacific Ocean

IMPORTANT CITIES

Moscow is Russia's **capital** and largest city. It is a center of history, business, and architecture.

Saint Petersburg is Russia's second-largest city. It is known for its history, culture, and architecture.

Novosibirsk is Russia's third-largest city. It is a center of manufacturing, transportation, and education.

Saint Petersburg
Population: 5.54 million
Moscow
Population: 12.64 million
Novosibirsk
Population: 1.69 million
RUSSIA
N
W
E
S
DID YOU KNOW?
Saint Petersburg was Russia's capital from 1712 to 1918.
SAY IT
Moscow
MOSS-ko
Saint Petersburg
SAYNT PEET-uhrz-berg
Novosibirsk
noh-voh-suh-BEERSK

RUSSIA IN HISTORY

People arrived in Russia thousands of years ago. Around 1240, Russia became part of the Mongol Empire. **Czars** began ruling Russia in the 1500s. In 1613, the Romanov family took power. This family ruled for centuries.

Ivan IV, Russia's first czar, was known as Ivan the Terrible because he was cruel.

The Russian people became unhappy with the country's leadership. They started a **revolution** in 1917. The last **czar** stepped down. In 1922, Russia and nearby countries formed the **Communist** Soviet Union.

Communism gave Russians little freedom. The Soviet Union broke apart in 1991. Russia worked to develop a new government.

Boris Yeltsin was the first president of Russia. He served from 1991 to 1999.

AN IMPORTANT SYMBOL

Russia's flag has red, white, and blue stripes. The flag was adopted in 1991.

Russia is a **semi-presidential federation**. The president is head of state. The prime minister is head of government. A legislature called the Federal Assembly makes laws.

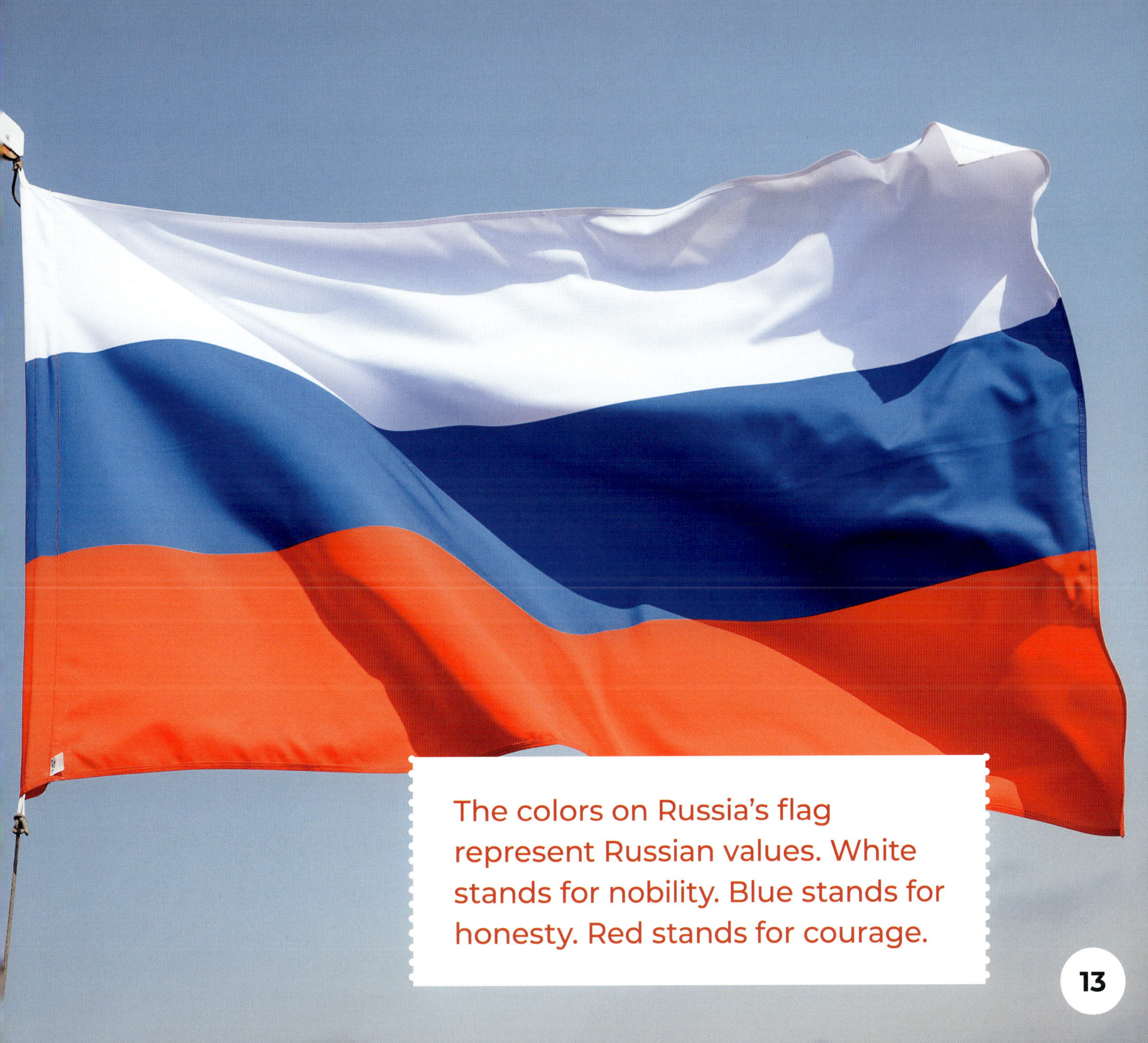

The colors on Russia's flag represent Russian values. White stands for nobility. Blue stands for honesty. Red stands for courage.

ACROSS THE LAND

Russia has **tundra**, forests, plains, swamps, rivers, and more than 200,000 lakes. The Ural and Caucasus are major mountain ranges.

Reindeer, elk, bears, squirrels, and lemmings live in Russia. Moss, berries, wildflowers, and many types of trees grow there.

Nearly half of Russia is forested.

EARNING A LIVING

Many Russians have service jobs. They work for the government or in schools. Russian factory workers make machines and clothing.

Russia's **natural resources** include gold, oil, natural gas, lumber, and coal. Farmers grow grains, corn, sugar beets, and potatoes.

Russia grows more barley
than any other country.

LIFE IN RUSSIA

Popular Russian foods include soup, pancakes called blini, and dumplings. Tea, coffee, and **kvass** are popular drinks. Favorite sports include tennis, ice hockey, and a hockey-like sport called bandy. Religious and folk holidays are important. Many Russians follow the **Russian Orthodox** religion.

Russians often eat blini during Maslenitsa, a holiday celebrating spring.

FAMOUS FACES

Yuri Gagarin was born in Russia in 1934. He became a pilot in the Soviet Union's air force. He joined the Soviet space program in 1960. Gagarin was then chosen to fly in the *Vostok 1* spacecraft in 1961. The mission made him the first human in space!

21

Maria Sharapova was born in Nyagan, Russia. She started playing tennis as a child. She began playing professionally at age 14. Sharapova has won many championships. She is one of ten women and the only Russian to win a Grand Slam.

Maria Sharapova
retired from
tennis in 2020.

A GREAT COUNTRY

Russia has beautiful land and a rich history and culture. The people and places of Russia help make the world a more interesting place.

Russia's Lake Baikal is the deepest lake in the world. It reaches a depth of 5,387 feet (1,642 m)!

TOUR BOOK

If you ever visit Russia, here are some places to go and things to do!

PLAY

Explore Sochi Park. It features Russia's highest and fastest roller coaster!

EXPLORE

Visit Novosibirsk Zoo. It is known for its many endangered species.

DISCOVER

Experience the famous
and luxurious Winter
Palace in Saint Petersburg.

WATCH

Russia is known for ballet.
See a performance at the
Bolshoi Theatre in Moscow!

RIDE

Take in the country on the Trans-Siberian
Railroad, the longest railroad in the world.

TIMELINE

1762

Catherine the Great began ruling Russia. She was Russia's longest-ruling female leader.

1945

World War II ended. The Soviet Union was a major power and fought alongside Great Britain and the United States.

1922

Joseph Stalin became general secretary of the Soviet Union. He would go on to become a powerful dictator.

1957

The Soviet Union launched *Sputnik 1*. It was the first satellite in space.

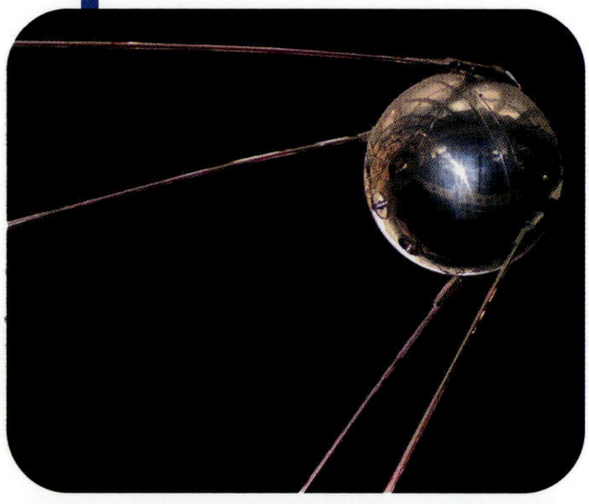

1991

The Cold War ended. This period of tension between the United States and the Soviet Union began after **World War II**.

2021

Fires destroyed a record-breaking 46 million acres (18.8 million ha) of Russian forest.

2014

Russia began the Russo-Ukrainian War and claimed areas of Ukraine.

2022

Russia invaded Ukraine, worsening the Russo-Ukrainian War. The invasion broke international laws.

RUSSIA
UP CLOSE

Official Name
Rossiyskaya Federatsiya
(Russian Federation)

Flag

Population
142,021,981 (2022 est.)
9th-most-populated country

Total Area
6,601,668 square miles
(17,098,242 sq km)
Largest country

Official Language
Russian

Capital
Moscow

Currency
Russian ruble

Form of Government
Semi-presidential
federation

National Anthem
"Gimn Rossiyskoy
Federatsii"
("National Anthem
of the Russian
Federation")

GLOSSARY

capital—a city where government leaders meet.

Communism (KAHM-yuh-nih-zuhm)—a form of government in which ways of creating wealth, such as land, factories, and machines, are owned by the state. They are shared among the people as needed. Something relating to Communism is Communist.

czar (ZAHR)—a male ruler of Russia.

kvass (kuh-VAHS)—a fermented bread-based drink popular in eastern Europe.

natural resources—useful and valuable supplies from nature.

revolution—the forced overthrow of a government for a new system.

Russian Orthodox—the Russian form of Eastern Orthodox Christianity. This is a Christian church that believes in saints and follows special traditions of worship.

semi-presidential federation—a government led by an elected president and an appointed prime minister and cabinet. The prime minister and cabinet are accountable to a legislature and sometimes to the president.

tundra—flat, frozen Arctic land with no trees.

World War II—a war fought in Europe, Asia, and Africa from 1939 to 1945.

ONLINE RESOURCES

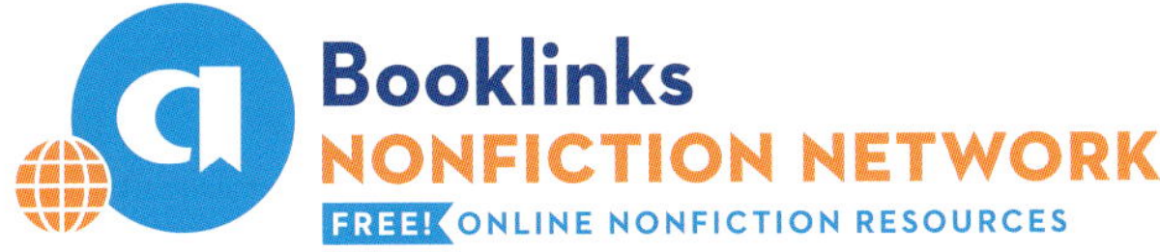

To learn more about Russia, please visit **abdobooklinks.com** or scan this QR code. These links are routinely monitored and updated to provide the most current information available.

INDEX